Just Chill

by

Ace McKay

PITTSBURGH, PENNSYLVANIA 15238

Dorrance Publishing Co
585 Alpha Drive
Pittsburgh, PA 15238
Visit our website at www.dorrancebookstore.com

ISBN: 978-1-6442-6572-7
eISBN: 978-1-6442-6595-6

This book is in love and appreciation to those who have walked this journey with me. Your faith, friendship and challenging words have meant more to me than you know.

I dedicate this book to my daughters Lennon and McCartney who have endured my hurts, habits and hang ups during their life. I love you both tons and I'm so elated to always be your Dad.

Introduction

This book will change your life!
I know that's a bold and dramatic statement, and it may or may not be completely true. The basis behind this book is to provide insight from my life lessons. If anything, it is an extension of my radio show where I share these kinds of parts of my life every day.

I have always tried to live my life from the perspective that I am teachable. If I stop learning life lessons, it makes me very anxious. So if it's God's lessons to make me better than I was the day before, then I hope even if you learn nothing from my life, if it gives you a filter of how to view your own life lessons, then it may very well change your life.

There are a million books for you to pick off the shelf or download, and all of them are full of life lessons from preachers, counselors, and trained life coaches that can help you better understand yourself. Trust me. I read them like they are going out of style because I am hungry to face the things I need to and not go through them in vain but to extract everything out of it that I can so that I don't repeat my mistakes, and as a follower of Jesus, I want it to be a way to bring me closer in my faith in him.

————

One weird and wonderful gift I have is the way I view certain things as God has shown me how He speaks to me. I see Him in sunsets and workouts and movie quotes and song lyrics. Sometimes I share my heart from these life lessons and people look at me like I have three heads and no clue. On the other hand, I have my "misfit" friends that appreciate the perspective because something about it makes sense in its own weird and wonderful way.

What I hope about why you picked up this book is that you feel like a misfit in this world, like you don't belong, and you are seeking to find your purpose or understanding for what to do next.

I'm not any form an expert, and I'm not done learning all that God has for me, but by the end of these chapters, I hope that you will feel comfortable in your own skin and realize your thumbprint on this world is by God's design.

If truth be told and its best you find out now: I am divorced, I cheated, I've lied, I've covered up. I've orchestrated things in my life for my gain, and I've lost focus on God on more than one occasion in my life. However, I am not striving to be perfect, but if something I endured or mirrors your life, I hope you can learn from my mistakes so that you don't have to endure what I did to get your life back on track.

Now don't get me wrong. I have no regrets because I have learned from these experiences, and God has redeemed and healed me from those moments. I'm not proud of the people I have hurt, but it's all still God's Plan-A for life to bring to where I am in life and in my faith in Him. It's also what brings me to writing this book, and if anything had played out any other way, I wouldn't be where I am or on the path to where I'm going.

If you've made it this far and want to keep reading then I'm excited about what God can do in your life as you see how He's worked in my life. All I want this book to do is to glorify Him and help you in your journey. These things didn't happen to me just for me. They happened to me for you as well, which is why I want to share how amazingly awesome God has been in bringing me though these valleys and the joy that comes in making Him famous.

If we can learn to be true to who we are and not just fit into the mold the world has for us in their agenda, we might just find true love, true joy, and learn to JUST CHILL!

Contents

Foreword by
Joshua Brown from Planetshakers

I remember the first time I met Ace McKay. The brisk, cold Michigan air nearly took my breath away as soon as I stepped out of the airport. I'd I flown half way across the country just to listen to what he had to say about music and the radio industry, and it was worth every moment. Anyone who's ever had the honor of meeting Ace knows he's full of creative energy, an outside-of-the-box thinker who seems to understand the ebb and flow of life like very few.

As a radio DJ, he's incredible. Every day listeners are invited to experience the ups and downs of his daily life through engaging, candid conversations filled with humor and wit. It's been said that perfection intimidates while compassion inspires. Ace understands that all too well and will be first to tell you he hasn't strolled through life untouched by tragedy, faults and failures.

Humble and transparent, he has a story to share. The question is, are you ready to listen? Through the pages of this book, the many layers of Ace's life will unfold. From enduring heartbreaking loss to devastating disappointments, you'll discover how seasons of suffering can shape your soul when you surrender them to Jesus.

So whether you've fallen or simply fallen apart, we all have a choice to make: stay stuck in our hurt or be renewed in our hearts. With deeply personal stories, Ace will encourage you to let go of the pain of the past and anchor your identity to the truth of God's Word. After all, being filled with the of beauty of His love will always bring out the best of who you are, freeing you connect with others, live with contagious compassion, and just chill.

Just Chill

"In My Mind and In my car, we can't rewind we've gone too far."

Video Killed The Radio Star - The Buggles

Chapter 1

On the Radio

As far back as I can remember, the radio was always on. When I was six years old, I took my headphones with me and hung not only on the music but the personalities behind the mic. What they said and did made a huge impact on me.

Growing up in Chattanooga, Tennessee, it was KZ 106. Moving to Birmingham, Alabama, it was KICKS 106 and Rock 99 or I-95, from legendary jocks like Brad Regal, Mark and Brian, and your friendly neighborhood "Birdman," who dominated my life and the airwaves at that time.

For any of the heroes we have ever had to look up to who inspired us, you understand that wide-eyed feeling when you see them, or in this case, heard them. Of course, being before the days of the internet and social media, radio was much more "magical" and shrouded in mystery. We never knew what they looked like, and when they were on location for live broadcast it was like Santa came to town with a bag of gifts.

For those of us that grew up in the eighties, going to the skating rink was a regular ritual. Anytime there was a Saturday, I was there as a kid. When Michael Jackson or Duran Duran was played, you knew I was out there at high speeds.

While the once-frequented Skate World is now a public storage facility in Hoover, Alabama, there was a school theme night when I was in the fourth grade. It was also really hyped in my mind because I got to go out on a school night to do something I loved. Walking in, the music was thumping, the lights seemed extra bright, and the DJ was hyping the crowd. He looked so cool in his retro letterman's jacket and Ray Ban Sunglasses. It was HIM! The Birdman!

He was just as crazy in person as he was on the radio. He had been this voice in my life that impacted me and made radio seem like the most amazing job in the world, and now here he was in the flesh. He was real! Now let me say this. I can say I'm been honored to meet celebrities in my life and to go backstage, but still to this day, my heart still races with excitement thinking about the night I met The Birdman!

The presence and vibe he had was so strong, and I didn't know then just how transformational it was until much later, but it was then that I knew I wanted to be a DJ.

— — — —

We all have those people in our lives that have made that kind of impact to set us on a course in life. You know that person you either admired or got to know through opportunities, who invested in the person you are today. It's quite humbling to think back to each moment and see how those little and big deposits shape us into better people.

We've probably all heard the phrase, "You should never met your heroes." In my life, I've found that to not be true. However, I've also seen my definition of hero change. It's not the people with posters, endorsements or million-dollar salaries that I look up to. It has become those who took time for coffee with me or allowed their true character to shine into the world. There are still artists, authors, or actors that I'd love to meet, but regardless of how close we ever get to meeting our heroes, we have a chance to take their nuggets into our lives and use them to better our spirits and hearts.

I heard actor Matthew McConaughey once say his hero was himself ten years into the future. I love that mindset, as it teaches us to not look up to other people but allow them or situations and experiences to shape us to be better than we were yesterday. If we are always teachable, the older we get we begin to see how we can learn from ourselves in the good, bad, and ugly moments. We become our own hero and also a hero to others as they see our character play into positive sides of life.

So much of our lives have us chasing things that don't matter. It's fame, fortune, respect, big houses, etc., that are distracting us from what really matters, and that's loving on people. I've never once heard someone in their later years of life wishing they had chased a better paycheck or fancier car. It always was about wishing they spent more time with family and regretting the missed opportunities in life.

As the Bible has guided my path since I was six, I know it has helped to shape how I see others, and God has instructed us to love others (Matthew 25:31-46). When we reach out to those in need or the hurting, we are showing a love for God that is lasting and goes beyond generations.

I have had my moments of regret as well, but there's nothing I can do to go back to change them. However, the sooner we learn that another bad choice or learned lesson is what makes us better, nothing is ever in vain. We learn to love others better as God intended because when you have been hurting, you just want someone to understand or show you grace. Well everyone is asking for that same grace in their lives.

As someone who grew up believing in God, it also ties into purpose for me. Others who follow after life with a Christ-like heart also understand that need for balance in life— that God orchestrates things for His purpose and NOTHING else.

Our actions and pursuit of life by the world's standards are nothing more than overflowed blessings if God chooses to give them to us. You didn't do anything to earn them. He gave them to you because He loves you. I've learned that in my forty years of faith, I refuse to look back on my bad choices as regrets because if I had done even one thing differently, I wouldn't have the blessings that I have and wouldn't be where I am in my walk with God. So given the chance to relive my life, I'd do it all the same.

We get passionate and worked up in pursuits, and there's nothing wrong with passion, or goals, for that matter. However it's how we treat people and love them in those pursuits that makes the journey even sweeter. All we have to do is JUST CHILL!

Just Chill

"Make This Dance & you'll look the best"
The Birds The Word - The Trashman

The Birdman

Chapter 2

The Birdman

Some days you just remember like they were yesterday.

It was a 1970's letterman jacket with a BIG "H" on it, Ray Ban sunglasses, and a personality that filled the room. That was the man, the myth, the LEGEND...THE BIRDMAN!

On the radio, he was funny and full of crazy stunts that just wowed and engaged people like myself to the point that you just wanted to listen to see what he would do next. Opening his show with "The Bird's The Word" by the Trashman let you know that the next few hours of your life were about to take you on a ride.

Once, he stood out in the freezing cold in his underwear to raise money for charity. Another time he was "arrested" on the air for being "too ugly" and listeners had to pledge money to get him out of "jail." These were crazy stunts that showed the heart of a man who truly cared about people and would give the shirt off his back if you just asked him.

– – – –

So as the night wound down, and all the parents, including mine, filed in to pick up their kids from the skating rink, we slowly paraded out the door. We were exhausted and winded from a great night with friends and with callouses on our feet from skating all night. I still remember my feet being heavy as they always did after going from skates on your feet to regular shoes again. It's like watching a toddler take their first steps; its takes a minute to settle in.

I was getting close to the counter by the door as we walked by where Birdman stood. Waving goodbye to the students who came, I just had to get close enough to meet him. I had no idea what to say or do. It was one of the few times in my life I was truly nervous. As we walked by, he leaned in and asked my name. As a kid I went by Ray, so as my voice cracked, I attempted to say it out loud. In the moment, he pulls his shades down onto his nose and looks at my mom, and with a loud YAWLP, screams… "Kathy?!" By the way, that is my mom's name, which blew me away because how in the world did THE BIRDMAN know MY MOM'S NAME?

The moment got even weirder as she looked at him, and with her southern accent screamed, "Bill!" to which I was floored, and my head began to spin, as I had no idea what was happening. Who was Bill? Why was this so-called Bill, aka Birdman, aware of my Mom and at this point in the night hugging her tightly?

What I soon learned was that not only were MY MOM and the BIRDMAN high school classmates, but they use to hang out ALL the time to the point that…HE…IS…MY…GODFATHER!

The rest of the night was a blur because I had tons of questions. I didn't even get to bask in the reality that I had just met my radio hero and icon! What followed that night was my mom telling me about all the times they did choir and hung out with their circle in the early seventies, which explained the letterman's jacket and the H because it was his actual jacket from Hixson High School.

My mom pulled out a photo album that I never remembered before that night. It could have been there, and I saw it but don't recall, but it was my favorite photo album after that because she had a handful of photos that were me at the age of two with a 15-year-old...BILL "The Birdman" Thomas.

Little did I know then how my relationship with Birdman would steer the direction of life in more ways than one.

– – – –

As a six-year-old little kid who was obsessed with music and the radio, I always thought, "What a cool job that would be" to play cool music, interact with listeners, and give away stuff on the air. I didn't think about the pay or wasn't even thinking about being famous. I just WANTED TO BE ON THE RADIO. It just fascinated me and as a kid and even as a teen, I never thought that I'd get that opportunity.

In the summer of 1991, I was 19. My brother comes home one day, bust in the door, and yells down the hall, "Guess who I just heard on the radio!" I was game, so I said, "Who?" He quickly responded...The Birdman!

My heart jumped like I had just won the lottery— not that I've won the lottery, I'm just assuming this is how it would feel. I asked where and when and jumped on the radio as he tells me KICKS 106, which in that day was a country station.

Now before I elaborate on this moment, you have to know two things. One, The Birdman had worked Birmingham several years ago and no one knew where or why. Later I would learn it was New Mexico because that's the industry. You go where the work is, so it takes you to places you never would have seen yourself living. The other part of this story is that I just moved back to Birmingham from Atlanta to actually take a shot at pursuing a career in radio.

Now I was too excited in that moment to think about my own opportunities. All I cared about was that my hero, my Godfather and MOM's BFF from High school was back in town and ON THE AIR.

So being a much more confident teen then I was at the skating rink a decade before, I called the request line, and unlike those moments when you call a radio station and they never pick up, He did!

My heart pounded as I heard his voice say, " Hi KICKS 106!" I quickly asked, "Is this THE BIRDMAN?" As he verified, he reciprocated sternly "Who is this?" When I told him it was his God Son, he screamed RAAAAAAAAY! What are you doing?"

Like any teenager on a Saturday, I wasn't doing much. He told me to come down to the radio station. I jumped at the chance because it was a dream come true. I mean it wasn't like after the skating rink event that we were palling around town or anything. However, to see a real radio station and hang with the Birdman was the be-all and end-all and still one of the highlights of my life.

— — — —

After several months of spending time with Bird, from being at the station to going to movies, burgers at Fuddruckers and watching Letterman late at night, Bird and I had gotten close. I had on several occasions given my spill on that he needed to hire me and put me on the radio. You would think he would jump at the chance to help his Godson get a leg up and pass the torch. He shot me down time and time again because he knew what his experience in radio had been and didn't want me to go through those hard times. Radio moves you like a military family, and sometimes new programmers are brought in and they have been known to clean house. He didn't want that for me, but I didn't care. I just wanted to do radio and was looking to get my foot in the door. After a few months back in Birmingham, KICKS had flipped to an "oldies" format, and Birdman was leading the way with a morning show and programming. So my drive to bug him got greater until one day he either was desperate or I wore him down. He made me commit to *every* Saturday night running "

Dick Bartley's Rock & Roll's Greatest Hits," which was a syndicated show, and all I was doing was pushing buttons, but I didn't care...I was finally IN RADIO! Now during the next two years of my radio journey, I was at Birdman's hip as often as possible. I wanted to learn everything I could and as fast as I could. I even recall my first radio name came from him, as we had been out DJing a wedding, and he was playing a Jackson 5 mix he had put together. I recall him saying, "This mix is so smooth they call me *Blades*." I screamed "That's it!" So for the next six years, I went by Billy Blades.

As Bird and I engaged in conversations about life, love, God, etc., he began to speak into my non-radio journey often. See, that guy that I told you about who did stunts on the air to raise money for charity really wasn't doing stunts just for ratings. He genuinely cared for others, but me being the twenty-year-old guy that I was, I was wound so tight I could pop out a diamond most day. I needed to relax and go with the flow more, so when life started to get to me, he would just look at me and say, "YOU HAVE to JUST CHILL!" He didn't just say it once. It was quite repetitive and necessary. It even felt like the soundtrack of my life was the Birdman remix song. In a life that we can't choose our DNA or family, you have the nose, eyes, and hair that was passed on to you. There are two things you *can* choose, and that's your faith in God and your personality. You may have elements that fit certain people you mirror at times or when you hang with them that part of your personality comes out, but who you become is based on the kind of person you want to become. Better that you become the kind of person God has called you to be. For me, I have adopted the personality, spirit, and passion that Bird had for life and others. God has tweaked it over the twenty-six years that he's blessed my life so that I still do radio to this day, which I still love as much as that six-year-old kid did. I'm not the only person with numerous stories of Bird's impact on their life.I close out my show the same way I host it, which is with the vibe that we have to let God define who we are. You can look up to people based on where they are in life, but God chisels down what makes you unique and how that makes you…YOU! This season in my life was the building block of who I knew I wanted to be as a true Follow of Jesus. Just like believing that radio was a good fit for my life, I was growing into the man God intended and not by losing myself in personality but in building the character He instilled in me and letting it radiate out in my life. I didn't know all that God had planned for that journey or how I was going to get there, but what I had to learn first was to JUST CHILL.

Just Chill

"I Know It's Only Rock and Roll…but I like IT!"
I Know It's Only Rock and Roll - The Rolling Stones

Chapter 3

It's ONLY Rock & Roll

Now to say that I love music is an understatement. I can't remember a time in my life that music wasn't playing, and most of memories are triggered by a song in some way. There was even a time that I couldn't memorize scripture well so it was songs with verses from the Bible that stuck with me best. My earliest memory of music was in the car with my Mom when it was her and I driving to Kmart to shop. The Eagles, Elton John and Captain & Tennille take me back there. Creed's *Arm's Wide Open* reminds me of the day I became a dad. Hall & Oats' "H20" album was the first time I bought music with my own money.As kids my brother and I had to rotate at times for who got the stereo in our room. We would take turns lying on the floor with headphones and blare whatever we were into at that time. Actually, sitting in my room and just listening to music is still a favorite pastime, and baffles most of my family and friends that I just "listen to music." As a vinyl collector, I miss the days of reading liner notes and lyrics and examining every inch of artwork on the cover. Streaming is convenient, but it has lost something for music snobs like myself. I still collect, as vinyl has made a comeback in the last few years, but there's just something about the smell and feel of a vinyl record that makes music really come to life for me.

In 1984, my brother and I had a neighbor who introduced us to contemporary Christian music, and while we grew up in the church, it was a Baptist upbringing in the South, so no guitars and no drums unless it was the Christmas Cantata, so it was hard for me to really identify with music on Sundays. However, it was a time for change in Christian music, and while Petra, Amy Grant, DeGarmo & Key, and Carman made my faith stronger through music, it was the release of Stryper's "The Yellow & Black Attack" that changed me FOREVER.

This was the time of hair metal in the eighties, and I knew I wasn't listening to stuff that was good for a teenage mind, but nothing else drew me in until this moment.

It was the first three songs on that album that I listen to nonstop for weeks. I knew every word, every lick, every drumbeat. It was explosive and what began my journey as a drummer.

For every Stryper album that came out until 1990, I was deeply rooted into the beat as a player and as a fan. The band's "visual timekeeper," as they call him, is Robert Sweet, and to develop my style I mirrored every lick of every song. My mom would even testify that every inch of my room was covered in magazine pictures of the band, along with posters and tapestries.

Looking back, I see now that God knew I needed something that engaged my faith more. I've learned through music that we each connect to God through a song based on where we are, and just like when you read a Bible verse and when you go back later and read it again and get something new out of it. Music does that for me. Again, I'm pretty sure most of the Bible verses I learned during that time came from CCM artists and their music.

Now I will also say that, proving God knows how to speak to us in song, He has also used secular songs to break through to me in times when He needed to get my attention. That's actually why my daughters are named after the Beatles, because at a time when I was not active in my faith and living my life my way, it was later albums like "Abbey Road" and early John Lennon solo stuff that spoke right into my bitterness and anger and brought me back to walking with God.

I'm not here to endorse secular music or tell you that only CCM or hymns makes you walk closer to God. I will say that as your faith grows, you have to have balance, and as God lives in your heart, you will learn to see the difference in your life based on what you listen to or what TV/Movies you watch.

I love that we live in a day and age that we can access music anywhere, anytime, and of all genres. If you like rock, blues, techno, new wave or even polka, there is more than likely a faith-based band that can feed that part of you, or better than that, your sight and view of the Lord. I love when we hear messages from Him in almost every song. I no longer have to spend hours at the local Christian bookstore looking for something that speaks to me. Sometimes the most unlikely song or artist might grab my attention as I live my life in a filter that looks for God in all things at all times. It took me a while to get here, but it's amazing to see Him in this light as He guides me.

I also love being able to go back to songs from my early faith as not just a reminder of what I have come through but also what new things can I learn with the lens I now have. Music is the true time-traveler that God gives as insight into where we have been, where we are, and where we are going.

— — — —

Now that I have gushed over my passion for music and its place in my life and the world, let me give you a challenge.

FIND YOUR ANTHEM!

There will be times in your life that you need those "Rocky" moments in not just championing you through to fight harder and hang on, but in times of celebration, worship, and even pain and hurt.

I have a couple of playlists I go to in each of these moments. Anthems I can cry to, scream to, and sing while giving God the glory to in each of those moments. The artists range from Skillet, Planetshakers, Lincoln Brewster, and of course STRYPER.

Not only does God know how to reach me in those moments as I sponge out those parts of my life that I want to let go of and the music helps my healing occur, but God defines me. So the music I sponge life through also defines my time too. You don't have to live your faith like everyone else. As a guy who's always been kind of a rebel, I have found rebelling against what other people think my faith and rituals need to look like is my cause to push forward in this book. Part of why I turned from my faith in college was because I got tired of people telling me how to worship and how to serve God and what to wear and how to look. WHAT? The Bible says we are created in God's image (Ephesians 4:24) and that God doesn't look at a person's exterior but what's on the inside (1 Samuel 16:7). It's your heart that God is after—that's it! The more you seek after God's heart, you become like Him, and then you seek after the heart of others by extending grace.

We hear enough from people on how you have to look like this or dress like that. You have to listen to this and protest like that. STOP LISTENING TO THEM! You are unique in Christ, and once you have accepted a life that walks in His steps, you aren't limited by what you can and cannot do, but you are FREE. Let the Braveheart cry now, "FREEEEEEEEDOM!" Don't get me wrong. There are God's guidelines for our lives so that we can live by His will, but how you celebrate Him and glorify Him as you walk that journey is between you and HIM!

I tell my daughters often, "to follow your peace." As you meet a "free will" choice in your day, where is your peace? If you follow that as the Lord guides you, you will start to see Him work and your faith grow.

Music may be that vice that helps you find your peace and your identity in your constantly growing faith, but as you rest in those peaceful moments you will find God teaching you how to JUST CHILL.

Just Chill

"Well I just heard the news today. It seems my life is gonna change"

Arms Wide Open - Creed

Lennon, me, and McCartney

Chapter 4

"Dadda Up"

Anyone who knows me or has listened to my radio show quickly finds out how passionate I am about my daughters, Lennon and McCartney. As a matter of fact, if we've never met, just asks me about them, and I'll stop what I'm doing and gush about how amazing they are. Lennon has her life all planned and mapped and loves God like no teen I've ever known, and Cart—or Carkei for short—she its hilarious and wants everyone to have as much fun as she does.

It was January 9th 2001, and Lennon Nicole came into the world. It was a whirlwind day, and I don't think I slept all night. I just stood at the nursery window in awe of the little, amazing child who was mine to keep and love and raise to the best of my ability. I can't help but tear up even as I tell you about that amazing day. Anyone who has ever been a parent would easily do the same, but they also might point out that it was in that moment (for me at least) that God showed me a glimpse of just how much He loves me.

I know that we will never be able to comprehend His love and its vastness, but the unconditional terms of it just blows me away and keeps me in check of the fact that He is crazy about me. He's crazy about

YOU too. I've given Him plenty of reasons and opportunities to give up on me…but He NEVER does. I would never turn my back on my daughter, and while I haven't always been the perfect dad, I would do anything for them, and they know it. Parenting is God's glance into what He is like for us too. He would do and does do anything and everything for you because of His love.

－－－－

When Lennon was two years old, she had this awesome habit; when I would come home or she would see me, she would come running and throw her arms up and say, "Dadda up!" Without hesitation, I would pick her up and love on her or take her with me wherever I was going in that moment. I've always done daddy-daughter dates with my girls, even as babies, but there has never been anything worth more than those moments when you hold your child and embrace them. We'd talk about what she'd been doing with her day. She'd want to have tea parties and play dress up, and I wasn't afraid to embarrass myself for the sake of my little girl's happiness. There was one birthday that I recalling eating at Joe's Crab Shack in Nashville when they asked me to ride around the restaurant slapping my backside while screaming, "Look at me, I'm a Cowboy and It's my Birthday" so I did, and the first thing out of Lennon's mouth when I sat down was, "Dadda do it again." I would have, too, but we got a free dessert, so there were other important, pressing matters at that point in the celebration.

The beauty in my investment into my girls is that I have seen them blossom into amazing young ladies, and as Lennon has gone on to start youth groups and learn to love people right where they are, she has a better handle on how to "adult" then I ever had. She's got her ambition in life set, and her faith is super strong.

She's overcome some major things in her life: depression, her parent's divorce, and moves all over the country, and with each thing she refuses to be defined by them but instead learns from them. Usually by the time she and I talk about something she's facing, she doesn't want Dad's advice. She has it worked out. She just wants to tell me what she's doing. I still speak into the moment, but it's usually met with a "I know Dad."

I always said that as long as I teach my kids about the Bible and The Beatles, the rest would take care of itself. So far so good, but I would say, I have learned as much from them as they have from me. Oftentimes Lennon likes to remind me that she parents me more than the other way around, and she may very well be right, but I will say this, that when I grow up, I hope to be just like her.

– – – –

Now as a parent, it's a very humbling time in our lives when we allow our kids to see our faults. I'm not proud of the fact that in my early non-chill days, I had the tendency to allow my frustration to get the better of me. I mostly had my blow-ups in private, but when you don't practice restrain in private, it's at some point going to surface in public.

I recall one particular summer afternoon when we lived in Florida. I took my girls to the pool, as I often did. The only perk to morning radio was having your afternoons free. Seeing that we lived in Tallahassee, we were 90 minutes from the beach, so pool swimming was the perk to a 75-degree day.

I was usually very careful to check my pockets before getting in the water because like anyone else, I didn't want to lose anything or have it sucked into a drain. On this day, though, I did not check first before jumping in because I was looking to race my girls into the water. As I cannon-balled in and my girls giggled with delight, I came to the surface quickly realizing my cell phone was still in my pocket. Now these were the days of flip phones, when it was smaller and less obvious, but it set me off because I was on call at the station and in the event of an emergency, I wouldn't get a call (and gone were the days of landlines).

I sadly did not allow my retrained nature to dominate, and my girls saw Daddy lose it.

As I did what I could to dry it out in a bag of rice, the phone was shot, and I soon found out that I was three days from getting a replacement phone.

After not only losing my cool, but as always in dealing with this necessary evil, I blew my afternoon with my girls because of it. That's a day I'd like to have back for sure. I mean, it's just a cell phone, after all. Why was I so hyped up? Looking back on it, the stress of the job that Bird tried to protect me from had gotten to me, and I'm ashamed to admit it.

Feeling defeated and ridiculous, I sat on the stairs with my face in my hands. It was then that I felt a four-year-old little palm on my leg. It was Lennon. In her sweet, soft voice, she said, "It's okay, Daddy. I get mad sometimes, too." I broke down and hugged her as the tears came down my face. I apologized to her and gathered myself in order to redeem the night with them.

That night, as I reflected and prayed about my actions, it was then that I came to the conclusion that I wanted my girls to see Daddy fail. How else could I show them how to handle these kinds of moments? As parents, we can't just be proper all the time. The more real I have been with my girls, the closer we have gotten, and the lessons learned are more open as I admit my faults so they can learn how to deal with their flaws as well. Some of the life choices I've made have affected them, and I was like most parents who wonder if they screwed their kids up because of it. I had a good friend in Grand Rapids remind me that God has them on their own journey and would use these life lessons to teach them things that would draw them closer to Him just as they had me. Again, God knows all and is not stirred by anything we do or don't do.

– – – –

My baby girl McCartney was born four weeks premature in September of 2003. With no fluid and the cord around her neck, she was an emergency C-section. That also was a life lesson that God used to bring she and I closer together, strengthening my faith in the process.

If you have ever been in the NICU with a baby, you understand how out of control you feel. All the tubes and monitors and the incubator that helps them build their strength just shows a real test of endurance and faith when you see them fighting for their life. Now I know Cart's four weeks is nothing compared to what you or others go through; I saw babies at one week and can only imagine what their parents were facing in those long months ahead.

With each day that her O2 level wasn't above 90 percent, she was in the NICU for a whole additional day. This is the stuff that they don't tell you about in the "What to Expect" books we all have read to prepare for our bundles of joy to enter the world.

Day one, her level was down. That became Day two. Day three which became Day four which tried my patience. I got really good at washing my hands and arms up to the elbow, so as not to get her sick from germs. All I wanted was for my baby to be okay and come home.

By day nine, I entered the NICU ready for more bad news and more waiting, but the doctor came in and she had sustained levels at 90 percent for long enough that we could take her home! Praise the Lord! I think I shouted a little, in my head at least, if not out loud.

Now her coming home did not mean she was out of the woods. She spent the next several years having to have breathing treatments every three hours, and any viruses she got only went straight to her lungs for about the following eight years.

I will say that as I look back on those days, it was scary, but God used that as a time to show His faithfulness. Looking at McCartney now, you wouldn't know she ever had any health issues. She doesn't have any residual problems, and I praise God for that.

Her early start in life has stuck with me though, as we all go through an incubation period in life. Sometimes when we lose focus or forget to breathe properly, God puts us back in the incubator so that we can get stronger. Sometimes we see it as we are being punished for something we did wrong, but really it's God's way of loving us. He pulls us out of fires all the time so that we can find sanctuary in Him. Some incubation periods are years and some just weeks or days, but no matter the hurt or damage that needs to be rectified, God loves us so much that He wants us to gain the strength we need to move forward in our life.

If you've ever met someone who has been through a rough season in life, you might be shocked to learn what they went through because to see them now, you would never know anything like that ever happened. That's God! He worked it out.

As hard as it is, and I'm speaking from experience on this, we have to allow those NICU moments to happen to us and others. We can't walk everything to the edge and leave it unless we walk it with God, and often times, just giving people space and prayers as they walk out their stuff is the best thing we can do.

The gift in those incubation periods is that we get to see God working, and it strengthens our faith as much as the others around us. Pain is not meant to break you apart but to make you stronger so you will be ready for whatever else you will face on life's journey. Pain comes to us so that we get stronger in order to endure more pain in life. The habit to create is to give it to God. Your feelings are valid, and God understands and knows what you are facing. I have started seeing painful moments as a badge of honor that God knows I'm ready to face, and like a muscle working to get stronger in a workout, the heart muscle needs to get stronger as well.

－ － － －

After several months of the "Dadda Up" ritual, I came home as I always did one day and there she came with her little feet a running. "DADDA UP," and it was in that moment that I felt God reveal to me that *that* is how He wants us to come to Him. Proverbs 18:10 says, "The righteous run to it and is safe and set on high," and I've found that since then, when I run to God with everything I have and with joy like a child eager to be held by their Dadda, I have nothing to fear.

Lennon and I have always had a close connection, and I believe it's because God has used her to teach me things about His love (Psalms 103:13). The reality is that God uses parenthood to show us His love, and He uses marriage to show us what oneness with Him is like (Matt. 10:32).

I know that you have been through some really tough and unfair situations in your life, and you have done things you aren't proud of, but don't forget: God is crazy in love with you. ALL He wants you to do is RUN to Him. It doesn't mean it won't be hard or frustrating, but He fills us up when we are lonely, and picks us up when we ask Him to. He carries us through the valleys and shows us how to live closer to Him as we get out on the other side of those hurts.

I miss those days of picking up my girls and just holding them tight, but if they have taught me anything in my eighteen years as a Dad, it is that when we run to God, He helps us to JUST CHILL.

Lennon and McCartney at a Pacers game in Indy around 2012

Lennon and I

McCartney and I

Just Chill

So I've started out for God knows where, I guess I'll know when I get there."

Learning to Fly - Tom Petty & The Heartbreakers

Chapter 5

The Hardest Day of My Life

Often when I describe myself to people, I say "I'm a man of many sides." That's not just a pun, it's a reality, and I can confirm that in my life it took My Heavenly Father, My Two Earthly Fathers and My God Father...The Birdman, to make me who I am today. They helped to shape the clay of a man that I am. With their life lessons, the personality, their hearts and even their flaws.

When you are a teen, you are looking for your own identity, and Birdman filled in the places of my personality that I had been looking for at a time when I was looking to step out as an adult.

Now don't get me wrong. I knew he had flaws and wasn't perfect, but it was the vibe he brought into a room—you know the kind of people I'm talking about—that just fills the room. That was Bird! He would be the life of the party and the party all at once.

While there were only about two years of our life together when he was back in Birmingham, they were pivotal in my life because he really did help me to learn how to chill.

Now one of the flaws that Bird had, which is common among radio guys, is to make plans and then something would come up with station requests so he would have to go work a weekend. Or the station was off the air so he would have to stay around to get it corrected. So on more than one occasion, Bird would make plans with me and vice versa, and He would get caught up in something at work. Yes, I would get frustrated, but it was my hero, so you quickly forgive and look forward to the next hang time.

In 1994, Bird was back at one of the stations he was at in his early career, WHHY in Montgomery, AL. It's a heritage station, and he was just as big there as he was in his days in Birmingham. Even though he was only an hour or so away, I was in school, playing in a band, and working at the station, so we both had plenty of excuses not to see each other.

One Wednesday, I got a phone call, and it was Bird!

As I answered, "Hey, whatda ya doin'?" he said.

"Hey Buddy! What's going on?" I excitedly expelled.

"I want you to go pick up Mitch (Bird's son), and you guys come down, and we have a guy's weekend," He quickly responded.

"Sure," I said.

"Cool, I'll call ya later with details, and I'll see ya Friday." He closed every call with, "I love you to death. Okay Bye."

Bird was always quick to be on and off the phone. Anyone who talked to him on the phone would make it a game to see who could get off the phone first because he was just so quick about it.

Well the weekend had been preordained, and I couldn't wait. It was a rare weekend that I didn't have any gigs or shifts at the station, so it was perfect. So Thursday came, no calls from Bird. Friday Came....still no calls from Bird. To be honest, as a twenty-one-year-old who had not yet fully learned how to chill, I was upset and decided to just make plans with my friends because apparently something came up and he couldn't hang out, so I just blew it off and moved on with my weekend.

Saturday morning came, and at around 6:20 A.M. my phone rang. I was still in college and living with my parents at the time, so I don't know why I was the first to answer the phone but I did. It was Bird's Sister Roberta.

"Hey Hon!" she said.

"Hey what's going on?" I said, still kind of waking up.

She softly said, "It's Bill, sweetheart. He's in the hospital, and it's not good."

My heart sank! I felt guilt for being mad he never called. I felt bad that he was in the hospital and I didn't know how bad he was.

Ya see, one thing I hadn't told you was that he battled cancer for most the time that I had him in my life. It had been in and out of remission, but apparently when he moved to Montgomery, it was back, and it took over quickly.

For anyone who has faced cancer in your family, you watch yourself or the person going though it lose themselves and change physically and emotionally. Bird only ever told a few people how bad he felt, and I wasn't one of them. He wanted me to see him as I always did. He always loved the place where our relationship was, and I'm sure that as a nineteen to twenty-one year-old, I just took his word for it that he was doing great and fighting it, so we moved on and never swam in the conversations of cancer for long.

So back to the phone with Roberta. She followed her statement with, "The doctors say they don't understand how he's still hanging on. The cancer has taken over his body, but somehow he's still hanging in there, and I believe he wants to say goodbye to you," she concluded. As I began to weep uncontrollably, I fell to the side of my bed as I realized what was truly happening.

As I pulled myself together long enough to write down where he was and to wake my folks to tell them and say we have to go. My mom and I just held each other in the hallway of the house and cried. She had known him far longer than I had, but his impact was profound and lasting.

I remember as we rode to the hospital, I just began to pray that "If God knew I wasn't strong enough to see him go, then take him home before I got there," so that not only was Bird at peace but so that closure could begin.

As we arrived, the tension grew as we got onto the elevator. The doors opened, and there front and center sat Roberta and one of his other sisters Ruth waiting for us. Roberta popped up to hug me, and as she did, she whispered, "He's gone Hon." I lost it! While my prayer had been answered, even now I can never tell this story without a flood of tears. **It was the worst day of my life**. I had never lost a parent or even a grandparent at that point in my life, so this was devastating in every way.

The closure of that day and chapter of my life with Bill "The Birdman" Thomas was also a birth of something else. I was bound and determined to keep his legacy alive, not only in radio, but in how he loved others.

Like I said before, we get to choose the personalities of the people we admire and that shape us into the people we want to be—or better than that—the person God intended for us to be. On most days of my life, on and off the air, It's a combination of him and my heavenly Father that makes me who I am.

We still have untapped potential in our hearts as we not only learn to love people but as Bob Goff says, "We become love" in this life. A seed of grace and a daily application of it will birth the fruit of how we should love the world.

Everyone is hurting from something, and it doesn't take much to often times trigger that pain. So when someone goes off on you or gossips or bullies you, it's because the thing behind the thing is that they are hurting and are looking for relief from it.

There's not a day that goes by that I don't think about Bird and miss him terribly. As radio has changed since his passing, I would love to know his thoughts. He was always creative and passionate about connecting with his listeners, and at times, radio seems stale and routine and could use a Birdman right about now.

He lives inside the hearts of those lives he touched, and when I see the alumni of radio talent that was honored to have worked alongside him, we're always full of laughs and stories as we remember how wild he was, but above all else, how he loved being on the air every day; it's a contagious passion many of us still hold to this day.

God has shown me through his eyes and Bird's actions that we are to just love people where they are; Especially our enemies. The only way love can exist is through grace, and by extending grace to others, we hope they extend it back to us when we need it. It teaches strangers and family that this is what I want to be known for: how I love and how God wants us to love.

We can't show grace to others without God in our lives, but I've found that once we surrender to His will and his vision, He brings people into our sight as He sees them. Not just as broken and bruised but as mendable and with the greatest of potential. That's how He sees you, and with an ounce of grace to the world, we all begin to learn how to JUST CHILL.

Just Chill

I know that Jesus ain't worried 'bout tattoos and cigarettes Or if you wear a golden cross around your
neck What about loving your neighbor and giving to
the poor I just want to love like that and nothing more
The Mystery Rhett Walker

Chapter 6

Tattoos & Cigarettes

There's nothing wrong with being a Christian and having a tattoo. I know that saying it will be met with controversy, but I'm saying it anyway. Just so you know, I have eight, and they all were after I became a Christian.

I was honored to grow up in a Christian home. Growing up in the South, the Baptist way was that you were at church every time the doors were open. Every Sunday, every Sunday night, and every Wednesday night, which I didn't mind so much because usually it was met with a buffet in the fellowship hall that was better than any Thanksgiving I could remember. I was at every VBS and Sunday school class imaginable, and later it was summers at Shocco Springs Youth Camp that were the foundations of my faith.

At any time did I see a Christian with a tattoo or hear of any approval that said it was okay to have one and believe in Jesus? No! It seems foreign now, knowing that so many people have them and profess to be a follow of Jesus. I've heard the verses in Leviticus 20:28 that proclaims an argument against it and the verse in Isaiah 49 that might say it's okay.

Honestly some people get them before they come to a belief in Jesus and others use them, as do I, to open doors to their faith so people can boldly hear about how God transformed them.

All eight of mine tell a story of faith, and I love when someone ask me about them so that I can share how God has brought me through those tough times. They also represent the character that I want to radiate at all times so that I represent God the best way I know how. So you could say my tats are also my accountability.

My first one is a Chinese symbol for music. As a musician and a radio guy, I thought, "If I only got one ever, I want it to represent something that is a major part of how God shaped me, and music has been quite the chisel."

Like most people who get tattoos, you don't ever stop at just one. They become fun and creative. So a year later I got my second, which staying in the theme of the first, it is a Chinese symbol for love. There's barbwire around the symbol, which reminds me that we have to protect those we love, but the points inside are a reminder that love hurts sometimes but it stretches us to love unconditionally and with brutal honesty.

Another is my Spade, which having the nickname Ace made sense, especially in seeing how God has used that name to open doors in radio, music, and writing. I told you that Bird named me Billy Blades, but when I moved into Christian radio, I changed, and at that time Ace McKay sounded like the cool night jocks that I use to listen to, and knowing I would have teens listening, I wanted to invite them into my show, so that's how it stuck. God named me, I guess you could say. In all fairness, the Ace came from growing up a KISS fan, and BJ & the Bear was big when I was a kid, so BJ McKay brought the name to life.

The other side of my arm is my tribute tattoo to The Birdman. The last chapter explains that well, I believe.

One of my favorite tats is the cross on my left arm that has tribal symbols on them that translates into "Faith Without Walls." Even though I grew up Baptist and still serve the same and only God, I don't want to be told how to worship Him, talk to Him, celebrate Him, or dream of how He might work in my faith. I want no limits to our faith for both you and me. It's not about the rituals of religion but the relationship and conversations we have with God every day that defines our life and our abilities to grow. The more unique my faith is to me, or to others too I suppose, the more freedom I feel in Him to fulfill my purpose and calling in life.

I have a flame tattoo that fills up most of my right arm. The meaning is simple and true. I walk through fires every day, but God helps pull me out before I get burned. Now I'd like to tell you that I haven't been burned before, either by someone I trust or by even my own actions. I have been burnt too many times. The tat also reminds me not to dance with the flames to see how close I can get before I get singed, but to run the other way so as not to be pulled in to the fires of temptation, pride, or selfishness. I don't even want to be associated with the flames for that matter. Sins of my past don't define me, but I also no longer try to tame them myself. Complete surrender is the only way not to get burned again.

The *Fireproof* tat on my leg was at a time that I was doing marriage ministry because I wanted a "fireproof" marriage, and that movie was the springboard for what I was doing at that time. Now those flames I said I needed to run from, I didn't always run. Sometimes I jumped in and didn't care about the consequences, and I paid a heavy price. However, the tattoo is very much close to my heart because I one day hope to be married again, and I want to practice "fireproof" living now so that I don't have to adjust in order to be committed or godly in my relationship. If I'm disciplined now, then I can just keep doing what I've been doing to be "fireproof" in all aspects of my life.

I saved the last tat I got for last because it probably gets the most raised eyebrows. It's a skull that's melting, and it's on my bicep. The idea came from an image I saw on a railroad track beam. Now it was rusted, so I believe that it just happened to take on the face that resembled that of a skull, but it may have been nothing more than that before. The idea of this for me represented the sin in my life that I want to melt away daily. I am not and won't be defined by the sin in my life or the baggage that I once carried. It took me many years to see this, but if God has forgiven me for something I had surrendered to Him, then I know it's melted away.

There may be some who knew me at my worst and want to always see me in that darkness, but for you and for me, we are defined by who God says we are—*not* by the world.

I love sharing about my tats and the lessons I've learned, and I even more so love to hear from others as well. I often will see someone with ink and stop them to ask the story behind it. Even if it's a great piece of artwork or there is an actual faith angle to their ink, it's a way to invest and connect with people. Taking an investment in them is meeting them where they are.

You can agree to disagree with me on if it's okay in God's sight to have a tat or not. I do know that it's not a salvation issue, so you won't go to hell if you get one. However, tattoos are a way to express yourself, and if that's something that allows you to do so, then go for it. On the other hand, tattoos can also be an idol, so check your heart with each one and love others more then you love your ink.

(Side Note: My rule of thumb on what to get is that if I think about it for a year and after that I still want to get it, then I do).

– – – –

As a kid and teen, I tried smoking, but it never was anything that lasted very long. I even smoked stogies in my thirties, which I enjoyed to relax, until I did my first "Insanity" workout, and that stopped cold turkey.

I will say that the only time I smoked cigarettes was in an effort to try to fit in and be cool like the other kids. Peer pressure has a way of doing that, ya know?

I've found in my faith that God has made us each unique. If I'm busy trying to be like everyone else, then who is being me? Who is going to fulfill my calling if I'm not? Who's going to fulfill your calling and purpose if you don't take your unique plan and identity and allow God to use you for His kingdom?

It takes us a while to get here. It took me a while to gain this kind of focus because I've very much been an orchestrator in my life. However, letting go and letting God work in our lives and through us, we finally will be learning how to JUST CHILL.

Just Chill

"Make my way back home when I learn to fly"

Learn to Fly – Foo Fighters

Chapter 7

Misfits for Life

Radio gives the opportunity to move around and live in places you wouldn't have gone otherwise, and one of those places I loved calling home was Grand Rapids, Michigan.

Now I didn't enjoy the winters and snow shoveling. I mean, I grew up in the South, where the smallest amount of snow shut the city down and every ounce of bread, milk, and eggs are removed from the shelves as people locked in like bears for the winter. So as I grew to deal with the heavy amounts of snow, I fell in love with the city and the people.

During that time, my daughter Lennon got me involved as an adult worker for TEC (Teens Encountering Christ) after I saw how TEC transformed Lennon's heart and mind in her own faith and gave her a great group of friends like I've never seen. The idea behind TEC is to bring kids closer to God by sharing what you've been through, and these kids love on each other beautifully, and I knew I wanted to be a part of that.

I'd like to tell you that my involvement was in speaking or teaching, but no, it was in working in the kitchen or playing worship, and really I was told that the adults really aren't supposed to work, just supervise.

So that's what I did. I was supervising and making sure they didn't burn the place down.

It was during that time that I met Terrance. This guy was loud and obnoxious, even by most people's standards. He even was getting in trouble with the other adult leaders, and my first impression was get this guy out of here. As I began my TEC journey, I just observed and jumped in where I felt I was needed or asked to do. Also, I told myself, "Don't hang out with Terrance if I want to not get in trouble." After all, I was there to serve, not stir things up.

As TEC continued, I found that in my down time Terrence was always around. You could hear his laugh bellow through the halls of the church, and the kids really gravitated toward him. Watching him invest in them was great, I must say, because it showed his heart, and that side drew me in.

Terrence and I started to get more acquainted as the weekend rolled along, and by the end of the weekend, I discovered that he had become my favorite TECie—and soon after, my best friend.

Another side note: He knows this story, so I'm not saying anything he doesn't already know. As a matter of fact, with the very next TEC, I found myself being as loud and obnoxious as he had been, and we were both getting in trouble at times. We also managed to get our own room together away from the other adult workers. Score! However, you can't deny the hearts of why we were serving, and it was always for the kids.

－ － － －

TEC is a quarterly event for West Michigan teens. So four times a year, high school teens have a chance to invite kids to TEC and also work and serve something bigger than themselves.

After a couple of TEC's, another adult worker joined the crazy force that TEC parents deal with after their kids passionately says, "You have to work TEC MOM." That's exactly what happened for Kasey.

Her son Simon had been through the TEC before the one she worked, and she fit right in. As a youth leader in her own church, it was like comfortable shoes for her. Even though she would tell you she felt like a fish out of water. Also, for anyone who has been involved in youth ministry, you know it takes someone who's a little off center to heed the call. I mean, locked up in a church for 3 days with 150 high schoolers is a special call for sure, but Kasey fit the roll beautifully.

Terrence and I quickly took her under our wing and showed her the ropes, but we also realized she was one of us—loud and obnoxious! By the second or third TEC together, my daughter Lennon rolled her eyes whenever she knew the three of us were working together or even hanging out outside of TEC. She said, "You guys are like misfits for Jesus." YAS! To get an eye roll is every parents dream. To know that my kids do not only love my friends, but they allowed me to be the crazy Dad they knew I was made to be was even sweeter.

So quickly the term MISFIT was embraced around Terrence, Kasey and me. Actually we are even considering a tattoo to represent the "three-braided cord" that God has formed among us. Watch out, it's coming.

The reality is, MISFIT is what we all are. The Bible speaks in John 15:19 that "we are in this world but not of it," which in my mind says we are misfits. We are not supposed to get comfortable where we are, but to warm up to our future in heaven. You can be loud and obnoxious if you want. If nothing else, be passionate about what God is doing in your life.

For those that have seen the musical *The Greatest Showman*, the main theme is unity among misfits—taking what is unique and celebrating it.

One of my favorite numbers in the movie is the song "This Is Me." The whole song is the anthem every misfit has ever felt, and it is the cry we all have when we just finally get comfortable in our own skin and no one is "Gonna stop us now."

I am not a stranger to the dark
Hide away, they say
'Cause we don't want your broken parts
I've learned to be ashamed of all my scars
Run away, they say
No one'll love you as you are
But I won't let them break me down to dust
I know that there's a place for us
For we are glorious
When the sharpest words wanna cut me down
I'm gonna send a flood, gonna drown them out
I am brave, I am bruised
I am who I'm meant to be, this is me
Look out 'cause here I come
And I'm marching on to the beat I drum
I'm not scared to be seen
I make no apologies, this is me

Being a misfit is also about not casting judgment and accepting people where they are and where they are going in their journey with God. The reality is, we all have done dumb things, and we have been rejected for those actions, so a redeeming Savior proves that we get second chances to show what happens in a life with Christ.

Terrance and Kasey were that for me, and because of my past they loved me anyway, just as Jesus does. We celebrate each daily. I love them both with all my heart and would easily be by their side in a heartbeat. While I have close friends around the world, at the risk of sounding like a teenage girl, they are my besties for sure.

This chapter is not about me gushing over my love for Terrence and Kasey, but it is a challenge to you to embrace that you are a misfit and that God may have put those people around you to accent and love you well.

If you don't have those people in your life, start praying for God to fill your wagon with the right people, and every wagon needs a few nuts, so it might as well be you.

You don't have to carry your past with you, and we all need those one or two people to walk alongside us in this life to pray for us, get rowdy with us, and love us as we are.

I find that I go through major withdrawal when I don't get some regular "misfit time," so if you are restless and need some of your own, it may just be what you need to find a way in your life to JUST CHILL!

Just Chill

"If my wings should fail me, Lord Oh please me with another pair"

In MY Time of Dying - Led Zeppelin

Chapter 8

Insanity!

I was a skinny kid. I probably weighed 125 pounds from sixth through 12th grade. Now I was pretty active with band, working in a grocery store, and just having that killer metabolism that most teens have. Oh how I miss it.

Working in radio causes you to work crazy long hours or weird overnight shifts, and when you couple that with the laws of nature, I found myself up to 185 by the time I started working in Tallahassee shortly after my youngest was born.

Now I'm not saying that 185 is overweight, but it wasn't me at my healthiest, and I wanted to do something about it. I began to eat smaller portions and did a slight workout, but it still wasn't me giving it my all. If you've ever started a workout routine, you know full well what it's like to feel very out of shape in the beginning, which I did, and finding the motivation to stick with it was just not clicking.

After a few years and following my divorce, I began to realize just how out of shape I really was. Not just physically, but emotionally and spiritually.

– – – –

It was the Summer 2011. I began to get serious about my health, and beginning the Insanity workout program was how I planned to do it. I did not know what I was getting myself into. The first week was a forty-minute workout six days a week that used no weights, just intense cardio bursts followed by a day of stretching.

The first few days I found myself coughing and screaming in pain as I was dripping with sweat by the end of the workouts. By the third day, my arms hurt, my chest hurt, my legs burned, and it was so intense that I would have to do the stretching DVD before my work outs just to loosen up enough to get through the workouts each day. I'm not a beach-body coach, so I feel I can call it like it is. It was *hard*!

As my stamina improved, I was feeling better by the end of the first thirty days. I could see the results, and it created the habit and routine of working out that I have been able to maintain since. I'm glad I don't have to do Insanity now, but I still want to maintain good habits so I can keep up with two teenagers and not snore anymore. My future wife will thank me later.

Those workouts challenged me, and the next thirty days bumped up to sixty-minute routines, but I made it through and was in the best shape of my life. I felt good and others saw the results to the point that they feared I was starving myself and kept telling me to "eat something."

– – – –

I don't tell that story to pat myself on the back or brag about how I look. If I'm being honest, when I think about my Insanity days, it is a reminder of the lowest time in my life. Not just because of how I looked, but I had made a series of bad decisions in the years prior that contributed to losing my focus on God, losing my job, getting divorced, and even worse, finding myself in relationships I never should have been in.

Those bad habits began toward the end of my first marriage and were part of what led to my divorce. Following my divorce, it was one Saturday night that had me in the floor of my living room in uncontrollable tears that was a defining moment in my turn around in my health, both physically and spiritually. I was unemployed at that time, and God continued to provide for me, and I began to find peace as I got my focus back. However, it hurt just like the workouts did in the beginning. I was so out of shape spiritually that it was exhausting. God takes us back to the mat when we lose sight of what's important, and that's a personal walk with Him.

It's not punishment. It might be aftermath of the debris we left behind in the wake of our bad choices, but it's exile for our training that He's really putting us through. I know it feels like punishment, and in those training moments, we find the desire to reach outside of what God is doing and find ourselves grabbing for something that feels normal or feels better than what we've been dealing with. I've been there and wore out that behavior too many times, but here's the reality of it all. We aren't alone in our training. We aren't alone in our pain. We aren't alone ever when we completely surrender to God's will.

You're training is God preparing you for battle. If we train well, then we are ready for the fight. We are ready for the challenges, and we are focusing on one true God who will guide us along every step. He can see the future and clear the debris out of our way when we go back into training. He will orchestrate the things that need to come together, even when we don't see Him at work.

God may give you visions or thoughts and passions for what He's leading you to, but it's rare that we get the spoiler alerts to what will happen in the end. As a matter of fact, I quite enjoy not knowing. His promises are consistent and true, but the joy of waking up each day not knowing when that door will be opened is such a thrill. Keeping good habits with Him and consistent in our prayers and conversations with God allows us to delight in him in all things and at all times. When we start to get weary from the training, we can cry out to Him, and He gives us the strength to carry on.

My friend and musician Tim Timmons reminded me last summer, "We are to seek first the kingdom of God." Tim said, "When bad things happen, who's kingdom is rocked?" I knew it was mine every time. We get worked up and the shock and awe of what went wrong was NO surprise to God. He knew it was coming, so if we seek His kingdom, then we don't have to be rocked by it. He's not waking up going, "What happened overnight?" He knows what's coming, and He just wants us to be faithful to Him through it all.

I'd like to tell you that since the summer of 2011 I've had it all together, but I'm still learning from all of that and have come to a great place in my faith by just surrendering it all.

The part that you may find as you let go of your past is that you had idols that took first place over God. I use to think my past decisions in relationships were based on TV and movies I saw, but really I was using relationships to define me and be my escape, and when they went bad or ended, I started looking for the next one to define me or to "redeem me" in some way. I'll say it again: "It's GOD who defines me, and His acceptance of me is what's going to fill me up." The same is for you too. There's nothing like God's love. He will show us what He sees in the mirror and guide us out of the dark places so that we can see what He has known all along, and that is that we have great potential to love others and ourselves.

I'd like to tell you letting go and letting God take control will be easy, but just like an Insanity workout, you will sweat, you will hurt, you will be challenged, and you will be stretched, but you will also grow in resiliency into the best spiritual and emotional state of your life. You have to dig deeper and keep going. When we love Him first, we then find a way to JUST CHILL.

Me with Christian Artist Tim Timmons

Just Chill

"So often times it happens that we live our lives in chains and we never even know we have the key"

Already Gone - Eagles

Playing Bass on the Worship Team

Chapter 9

Habits & Hang Ups

We've all had those jobs that we've had to work our way up the corporate ladder if we planned to make any good money or make a career at something. Radio didn't just happen overnight for me. I gave up lots of weekends and tons of sleep to learn and craft the art of on air personality and learn programming, promotion, and production skills. There's more to it than just opening the microphone and talking.

I can't begin to count the number of Sundays I worked split or double shifts, which often times took me away from church. Now I don't want to blame radio for interfering with my commitment to church or my faith. I could have made it work if I had been more disciplined. I say all that to point out that it was when I scored my first full-time radio job that I was finally working during the week and freeing up Sunday morning to get back into my routine of church attendance.

I knew after years of searching to find my own identity in my faith that I wanted to find a church that allowed me to use my talents as a drummer because I also knew that the music would be more contemporary then the style of music I grew up in.

Sure enough, the first church I looked for with a contemporary service, I called ahead to verify the service times and mentioned I was looking for a band with a drummer. As they concurred about having a drummer in their worship team, they asked if I played, to which I said, "Yes." What I didn't expect was as I walked in the service, I was met at the door by the person who had answered the phone, and she told me where the drums were. Yes! That's right, I was asked to play my first Sunday there. No rehearsal, and at that time worship music was a new thing, so there wasn't a staple of Tomlin songs in my catalog to be able to jump in on. It was a true test of ten years of playing as I slid in behind the kit while the keyboardist began. Now he didn't see me, so as he continued to play, I found the beat and just filled in where it fit. He turned around as he played to hold a big smile because apparently I was filling a void the church had been looking for.

I quickly discovered that if you just make yourself available to serve, God WILL use you.

Playing Drums in Grand Rapids

- - - -

After moving to Grand Rapids, I plugged in with the worship team for Kentwood Community Church. One of my songwriting friends asked me to come fill in one night on drums for the Celebrate Recovery worship team, which given my track record, was nothing new. I just went where God called me to play.

As we began to run through the songs for that night, the regular scheduled drummer showed up, which kind of moved me to percussion by default. I knew after that night that it was the heart of Celebrate Recovery that made me come to enjoy Monday nights because of its "misfits" embrace that it had for people. You were welcome to come as you are, leave your habits and hang ups at the door, and let your faith grow.

Now there had been about a handful of truly real moments that I remember hearing God speak to me. One was when I was eight, another was when I was called into music ministry, and another was that night playing in the Celebrate Recovery worship team. While I was driving home that night, I asked God how I could serve, seeing that I was already playing the drums for the Sunday worship team for multiple campuses, He clearly said, "You always wanted to play bass. Here's a place to be used." Now playing bass sounded excited, but I didn't have the money for a bass or even know how to begin. Within two days my buddy Sam gave me a bass he bought for his daughter that she didn't want to play. Hence, my passion for bass began.

Just like the church that put me on stage first time in, I was two weeks into learning, and the Celebrate Recovery band called again, but this time to come play bass. I wasn't nervous because I had nothing to lose, and I was called to play there after all, so I went.

Now I'd like to tell you it was magical, but it wasn't. I played the basics, and recalling the three songs, I'm sure I missed quite a few notes, but it didn't matter. God had opened up a new passion in me, and after playing drums most of my life, I was becoming a bass player truly ordained for the purpose of worship.

With so much more to learn, I still play, and much more than as a drummer I must say. As I made Monday a night of misfits with the Celebrate Recovery crowd, I have been finding it has become my favorite ministry.

Let me say, if you feel God is calling you, just do it. It will be the most rewarding thing you will ever do. It also is like the story in Matthew 25:14 about the men who were given "talents" or coins to invest. When you read it, it clearly tells you about How the talents were harvested and grew into so much more because they planted them well. It also shows you what happens when you don't use the gifts and talents too. If you are still trying to figure out that calling, just serve where you are, and I promise, God will bless you in those moments, and as He sees you being obedient, He will grow your territory and talents. Serve him where you are, and He will then take you where He needs you.

– – – –

During my time in Celebrate Recovery, it wasn't all just about the music. There was spiritual growth going on that I will never forget.

The faith-based program created out of Saddleback Church with Rick Warren has a track record of aiding people dealing with issues from addictions to hurts from divorce or co-dependency, along with other healing avenues.

Some of the baggage I walked into was from two divorces and a string of bad habits in between trying to either find true love or "make good" for the bad choices I had made.

Now let me point out that love is like baseball. It is oftentimes an error sport. You learn from past relationships to hopefully form good habits that you can one day take into a life commitment with someone 'till death do you part. However, the phrase in sports that commentators like to throw around when a stellar player is having an off night is, "He has a chance to redeem himself." There really is no way to redeem yourself in love or to make people see you in a different light. There's no redemption in sports either. You have an off game, but it doesn't make you a bad player. You have to let the bad choices go and learn from them, or you will be doomed to repeat them.

There are ways that God can teach us when we let Him, but if you are still waiting for love, I'll just be straight to the point much like I have been on my show about this. You have to be true to who you are in Christ, and the right person will be drawn to you. The habits and hang-ups you have going into the relationship will follow you. So choose discipline, wisdom, confidence, and good Godly balance, and focus on Him as a single so that you just keep repeating that behavior even after you begin to date someone.

We oftentimes lose ourselves in relationships or they become an idol or escape. I can speak firsthand that it's no way to go into a relationship because it will only cause you more hurt later. So surrender your search for love or your current relationship to the Lord, and let Him orchestrate things for you. Don't grow weary in the waiting because either you aren't ready yet or the person He is crafting for you on the potter's wheel isn't ready. It could be both. We should only want true love when God knows we are ready. Not when we think we are or NEVER when we are lonely. Why in the world would you want to drag some innocent person through your issues? Fix 'em! Let God heal you, and let Him be the focus so that you have joy no matter what you relationship status is. Besides, nothing is sexier than a godly person!

As a teen, my escape and need for something "adult-like" is what got me into bad habits that followed me well into my adult years, and it's insane to keep that cycle going. You won't find love that way, and the sooner we release our hearts to God, the sooner we can heal and be comfortable as a single because it's when we least expect it that He will introduce us to the "perfect-for-us person."

Listen, letting go of past hurts or keeping triggers from spiraling us around in relationships is so hard. The stringing of the heart and head, the thoughts that bounce around driving us crazy, in and out of relationships, is enough to make most of us never want to date again.

Just breath. Let God pull you closer to Him so that you are so attractive in Christ, the one who is going to be yours will not be able to resist falling in love with you. All you have to do is JUST CHILL.

Just Chill

"My Soul ain't what it used to be but my soul ain't what it's been."

Sirens – Casual Boss

Chapter 10

Barking Dogs & Sirens

If you grew up in a family neighborhood, you have probably experienced or been the home of the dog that drives the neighbors crazy. My parents have those kinds of dogs next door and always have.

You know the kind of dog I'm talking about. Rather than barking at intruders or scary situations, they bark at everything and everyone, so their "Chicken Little" approach to the backyard makes you never know what's really happening. As a matter of fact, you get them going with the dogs across the street, and it's like a barking orchestra that no one wants to hear.

In trying to JUST CHILL when the dogs were over the top, I found ways to deal with it in order to keep my sanity. So any given day as I walked to my car, once they catch sight of me, they spewed a series of barks that riled the silence of the morning. So I took on the act of being the dog interpreter, pretending I knew what they were saying.

Setting the scene: A cool brisk morning as the sun rises.
I walk to my car as the dogs wrestle.
Dogs: BARK BARK BARK

ME: Good morning boys

Dogs: BARK BARK BARK BARK BARK BARK

Me: I know I saw that on Facebook. Pretty scary stuff huh?

Dogs: BARK BARK BARK

ME: No, I'm not worried, God is in control.

Dogs: BARK BARK BARK BARK BARK

ME: Well good to chat boys, don't eat any weird sticks now.

Dogs: BARK BARK BARK

(…and scene)

I know my brain produces weird stuff all the time. That's just a tiny part of the misfit mind. Thanks for riding, I hope you buckled up.

As much as it started as a coping mechanism to help me not be frustrated by a couple attention-seeking pups, it made me aware of something. We all have those people in our lives, much like these dogs, that "yap" until someone pays them some attention or "yap" for the sake of noise. Maybe they gossip or blurt things out to people out of fear, pain, or out of feeling like they need to be right.

We all have a past that we'd like to forget, or better yet, that we'd like others to forget as well. Sometimes the yapping is in our direction or the yapping we are just as guilty of is coming from unresolved issues in our hearts and head. It's what I call the "Thing Behind The Thing."

Now I don't have to remind you that we can't change our past, but in saying it, don't forget it. The past is over, but if you have not yet dealt or faced the ramifications of the past, then you are either doomed to repeat it or will forever see yourself *as that person*. You can't change how others see you except through your fruit, and you can't bear good fruit until you deal with the view of yourself in your own head and heart, and you can't heal until you dig up the roots of what caused those bad actions or choices.

The biggest goal we need to set each day is to win the battlefields of our minds. The enemy only knows your past, so he can come in and remind you, but if you give it to God and never pick it up again, you turn from those habits and hang ups. Then, even if they never choose to see your fruit, you at least won't be affected by the yapping from others because you will be closer to God, stronger in faith, and aware that you are now making wise decisions.

You may even face situations that are similar to your past, but when you have surrendered them to the Lord, the new common denominator is that in the same situation your actions will be different because your standard is higher and your dignity in Christ will help you react differently in that situation or know when to run from it before it affects you.

Now your past may be different than mine, and you can't relate to how I could have done some of the things I've done and still call myself a Christian, and honestly, I could say the same things about you. However, your past does not define you, and I hate the pain and emotions you have had to deal with that made life unbearable, but when you let it go, it truly doesn't define you, and the new you can shine. I've heard it said a million times, "Make 'em wonder why you're still smiling." That's the joy of the Lord that lives in you because what they don't know while they are busy yapping is that you didn't face those things in vain. We are supposed to learn from them, and as long as you learn and turn away from them, then it wasn't for nothing.

You took the hard lessons, and you not only put them into practice but also shared them with your kids, co-workers, small group, or whoever God needs you to so that you can help them avoid the same issues.

– – – –

As a writer, poetry has always been a great outlet for my emotions. I'm not afraid to talk about where I've been or where I'm going, but music and words help to sponge those moments out so I don't swim in them for very long.

My past has come out in many forms in songs that you may or may not ever hear, but one of the main ones that's been my anthem is a song I wrote with my buddy Adam Klutinoty from the band "About A Mile."

I use to pour out words into paper, and email or text Adam every Saturday, and when he connected with one, we would work on it together. You can actually find us in my basement performing this song if you want to hear it.

The main idea of the song *Siren* is that we often get called out into the water, like a mermaid to a sailor. The temptations and distractions of life pull us away from God and away from His purpose for our life. They can cause us to compromise our character or forms bad habits that we don't even realize until we are pulled under the water and about to drown.

This song is my battle cry for my life and yours.

V1
I'm losing all my friends
from all the wrong I've done
I wanna make amends
And replace where there's none

Bridge
Sometimes I got a fight to show them I know what's right
But I had to take the fall for Love to show me it all

Chorus
They'll be no more sirens
Pulling me away
I'm not going to give in
I know I need to stay

I see love through a clear lens and I and I never want to stray
So no more sirens

V2
I see the way they look at me
It pierces more than my skin
but my soul ain't what it's been but my soul ain't what it used
to be
Loves finally going to win
https://www.youtube.com/watch?v=bH6ZvgTwSTQ

The "sirens" in your life have to stop being your excuse for why you do or did something you shouldn't. We have to take ownership, live with the ramifications, and remind ourselves that the best is yet to come because we are still on God's Plan A. We are not and never will be strong enough to derail God's plans.

As we learn to let go of the past, our actions change, our hearts changes, and we can ignore the yapping dogs and the sirens. That's where real peace is found in the Lord and when we are finding the way to JUST CHILL.

Just Chill

"Fear of God and Fear of the rod will raise a Good boy"
Like Father, Like Son - Rick Springfield

My Mom & I

Chapter 11

Momma's Boy

Now one side of me that I have not confessed but am never ashamed of is that I am truly a "Momma's Boy." I've always been close to my mom, and many of my "heart on my sleeve" moments in life I attribute to her and how she loves people. She's the greatest mom anyone could ever have and still my hero when it comes to her faith and trust in God.

– – – –

On any given Saturday when I was a little kid, Mom would be in shopping mode, and as much as I can remember, she always took me with her. As a single mom, she didn't really have much choice; just to find someone to watch me at times so that she could work was a struggle enough. I think for people who have never been a single parent, you don't know how much a daily miracle it is to work and raise kids without losing yourself. It's more work than people admit when they are in it, and unless you have been there it's hard to really explain. We can only see based on our own experiences, but if you ever have a chance to help a single mom or dad catch their breath, I highly recommend it.

Now as an eager kid, I never met a stranger, and going to Kmart with my mom was always a treat because I knew that if I was a good boy, I'd get rewarded with a tiny bag of popcorn and a cherry ICEE. I think that's why to this day when I go to the movies, the reason it's my treat of choice because it still feels like a reward in my life.

Mom and I did so much together. We went to drive-in movies, we went to church, and we went to visit my grandparents and great-grandparents. I think back on that time in my life, and it truly feels like another lifetime. It was the routine of that life before we moved to Alabama that really was the foundation of my relationship with her, but it shaped a time in my life that seems so foreign. When I see the family members now that are left on my mom's side, we talk about those times in our life, but it's like watching a movie in my mind. Was that real?

– – – –

The thing I've come to love about my Mom—not just because she's my mom but as a woman of God— is that I've watched her struggle with her past and the words that loom large in her mind at times when others have put her down or judged her. She used to always says to me and my brother, "Don't let anyone tell you that you can't do something, and don't worry what others think of you. Just focus on what God thinks of you." That is the advice that shaped me so much and that I pass on to my daughters and anyone where it fits. As a matter of fact, when I've gone against one or both of those philosophies, I have lost sight of my purpose and worth.

We all know what it's like to be in those words and actions of our past, and I'd like to tell you that they go away, but they don't. What I learned from my mom and in my own faith has been that we surrender other people's thoughts about us when we surrender to God. His opinion *really* is the only one that matters.

Mom's strength in the Lord has always been strong, but it still didn't mean she didn't believe at times that her health problems or her placement in life wasn't somehow a punishment for the life choices she made. We all have doubts and at times disbelief in our potential or even in how God sees us because we think He sees us for our flaws, but He actually sees us for our potential.

I always saw mom in the mornings praying and reading her Bible. She would put on music and sing joyfully because even when she was battling those voices in her past, she knew God had redeemed her, and in the midst of her health problems, that faith was what carried her through it—and still does to this day.

The truth of the matter is that the only way you, like my Mom, can see yourself through God's eyes is by having daily time with Him.

— — — —

As I looked to find my own identity as an adult, so much of my early non-chill days were me rebelling against the traditions of my mom's faith because I wanted my identity in Christ to look different. As I've gotten older, while it may be different devotionals or styles of music from what Mom would have, it's still built on God's word, and it is that early morning quality time with God that has helped me grow in my faith. I'm a "touch and time" person, and God made me that way, so why wouldn't my time with Him allow Him to touch me and make me better and feel His love? When we make Him the priority in our heart, He clears the cobwebs and broken pottery around us. Because here's the deal: God's love for us and opinion of us is based on His purpose for our lives, which is first to have a relationship with Him, and the rest will fall into place. He didn't make it difficult to understand. *It's just simply that.*

My Mom's ability to raise me came out of her past and wanting more for her sons than she had—and not in stuff or money, but in faith. She wanted us to pursue God so that when life got hard or people put us down, we would focus on God and allow Him to heal us through it. She also wanted us to not be defined by what the church says you should do in rituals or in how people's opinions would weigh on you.

In my experience, only focusing on a relationship with God is so freeing, and the rest *does* fall into place. It may never fall into place as quickly as I'd like it to, but it *does* fall into place, and it's better than I imagined.

Failures help us much more than our successes. If we only see ourselves through success, we can get prideful and possessive, believing we are entitled to more than we have and to have it now. God takes our failures and shows us the life lessons, and it's in sharing how we got through those failures that allows others to understand His grace and goodness for their lives. We also aren't doomed to repeat them and hopeful helping others avoid the same pitfalls or judgments.

Mom has a sign in her bedroom that says, "Love Deeply," and it sums up who my Mom is in a walk with God. She loves deeply because she doesn't want anyone to feel unappreciated, and because God loves her, she wants to share that with the world. Sometimes it might be in a home-cooked meal or words of encouragement or a big fat hug, but she loves deeply.

I have been shopping with Mom enough times that I've seen her look people in the eyes at the grocery store, and she feeds into them in that moment to encourage them for a job well done. It's an amazing vibe to watch, and I find myself doing the same.

When you love others deeply and love yourself deeply it shows that by loving God first, you have learned how to JUST CHILL.

Just Chill

"When I cannot see, you keep my feet from falling. You
hold me in your peace, Here in the Grand Scheme."

The Grand Scheme – Solomon's Wish

Dad and I with my daughers in 2008

Chapter 12

Pride in Your Lawn

Being in radio, with each job I would move farther and farther away from home, which made holidays and visits very difficult. So when I got the chance to come to see Mom, I would take it.

Last Mother's Day I had the chance to surprise her as my brother Eric and I came into spend the weekend with her, and she had no clue.

As we pulled in the driveway, I could see her sitting at the kitchen table, and as she caught my eye, her "rest-face" quickly turned to excitement, and she screamed so loud that I could hear her through the windows into the street.

She ran out the front door and hugged me with the tightest embrace a son could endure from his Mom. I was close to a WrestleMania submission just to get her to let go because I was beginning to lose oxygen to my brain.

Once I broke the hug from Mom, as she reached to "choke hold" my brother, I saw my Dad walk out the door. Now I'd like to tell you that I remember his expression during this surprise, but really all I remember was how frail he looked.

See, Dad had been sick for quite a while, but I didn't really know by how much until I laid eyes on him. I don't recall my Dad ever having even the slightest cold when I was a kid, so this was breathtaking.

He had been battling reflux issues to the point that he had thinned out by over thirty pounds, and it showed. Honestly, he had never been a big guy, but he has always been active and healthy. He ate well and worked out daily. Even in his retirement, he works in the warehouse of his brothers' construction company a few days a week just to make sure he stays active.

If you have ever watched a parent or loved one get frail from illness or cancer, you know how devastatingly sobering it can be. I saw it in Birdman when I saw him the day he died but had not seen it in a loved since then.

Like most men, Dad never wanted to feel like he was a burden on anyone and wanted to still feel he had purpose and goals no matter how old he got. This was the first time in his life that I believe he ever had to ask for help or that people took things from his hands because he needed rest.

As I traveled that weekend back to Michigan, I began to feel God tug on my heart to come home. So a few months after that, God orchestrated a job so that I could come take care of my parents, or worse I felt, to maybe even return to say goodbye to my dad.

– – – –

If you've ever had to move back in with family after living on your own for some time, it's very humbling. There are adjustments in getting to know each other again and also in those moments of living as close to your normal lifestyle as you had before but only around other people. Wrong! It doesn't happen that way. If anything, it's the opposite. You are in their BNB and need to follow the rules. While you may not be a child anymore, there is a time of adjustments that have to be met with grace in order to see why you are there and how to truly help them.

I moved back with as little stuff as necessary, which in all fairness was clothes, vinyl records, and my laptop. I began to plan in my mind all the ways I could help my parents. I could cook. I could do the yard-work and drive my mom to the store and do laundry and dust, etc. I was set and ready to be there for them. What I quickly found was that by trying to take those tasks away from them, I was taking away their livelihood and was doing more damage the harder I tried.

While my heart was in the right place, it still wasn't really why I was there. We all seek value and worth in our lives, and the older we get sometimes we can feel less vital to those around us, so we need something. My dad needed his yardwork, my mom needed the house and loved to take care of the house and anyone who was in it. She is a southern woman and loves to cook you a Paula Dean-style meal so that she knows you ate well. That's what was a big shocker with my dad's weight because I knew Mom's cooking is amazing, so for him to lose thirty pounds made me realize something was really wrong.

As the weeks turned into months, I found that it was the emotional investment into my parents that was part of why I was called home—to get reacquainted with them as not just my parents, but as people.

While some mornings were them pouring out their hearts, some were me pouring out mine. I actually found myself giving them the advice in life or faith that they gave me as a kid, so the circle was coming back around, and it was so beautiful.

I heard them confess about things they regret that were very similar to those things I also was looking to let go of. See, I told you about part of the reason I came home, which was to help take care of my parents. The other reason was God sending me into exile to retreat from my life and a season where I lost my job due to actions of my own, and also to regain my focus on Him.

Those morning conversations were as much about God speaking to me as it was Him speaking to my parents. I began to learn that one of the habits and hang ups that I really had created in life was using relationships to be my identity in the world, and also I, like most of us, had been making decisions in the valley. When we hurt or try to "redeem ourselves," we choose to do things to give us relief or to show people that we are better or changed, but really we only make it worse when *we* orchestrate things.

Jeremiah 29 often is our focus when we believe God has a hope and future in our lives, but the further you read, you see that it's God who will restore you from exile and rebuild your reputation.

All I want is that when I lay down my head at night I know that I did my best to delight in the Lord in all things, and when I fail to go to Him, but when I succeed in that delight, that tomorrow I want to build on it.

When I first started in radio, I had a program director tell me to never chase the title or the paycheck. I needed to work where I felt I could learn from others, believe in the vision of the station, and feel I was contributing, and if any or all of those ever change, then it was time to go somewhere else. I believe the same goes in our faith. I don't want my relationship status, job, my role as a father, or my talent level as a musician to be what defines me. I want to be where I am as I believe and trust in God's vision for my life, learn from those around me, and feel that I have something to give—which I do—and so do you.

The sooner we can be confident that God is building us up to be confident in our skin and with grace become love to the world, we will begin to have peace and joy in our life that is so contagious. My mantra has been "Lord, use me where you have me and take me where you need me." It's total delight and dependence on Him.

– – – –

After ten months of being back at my parents, it was March Madness time and the day of the Final Four was happening that Saturday afternoon between Villanova and Kansas and Loyola-Chicago and Michigan.

As early as I can remember, basketball has been the core of my free time with my dad. We would go to UAB games as a kid, and when I later was a part of the NBA for a few seasons, I would take him to Pacers games, and it was fantastic.

So the day of the Final Four, we knew tip off was at 5:10, and Dad wanted to get the yard done because it was also Easter weekend. So I asked him if I could help so that we could get it done in time to watch both games. He with ease and peace said, "Yes."

We had a game plan. I would mow, and he would edge around the house and shrubs, and while I'm sure it's not the fastest a lawn crew may have finished, I felt that two hours for all of it was pretty good.

My dad had always taken pride in how his yard looked and how clean our cars were growing up. He told my brother and me once, "There's more to driving a car than just getting in it and going." That stuck, and I have always valued my cars and done the oil changes and tire checks, and I love having a pristine car.

So as I popped in my ear buds, as I had hundreds of times to mow that lawn, I loved it. Also, as I took the mower past the fence of the yapping dogs, I looked over at them because my verbal coping ways wouldn't have been heard over the loud, smoke-bellowing lawn mower. So I looked them square in the eyes and the yaps stopped as they ran away. It was a shining moment.

It wasn't just in cutting the grass so I could watch the game with my dad that night, but it was that I was serving him. I was helping to ease his load. I mean, truth be told, I'd just assume hire someone to do it than do it myself, but I was cutting the grass for my dad, and even with the high standard I knew we was expecting, I did my best, and when it was all said and done, I found myself sitting in the backyard swing with my TEC water bottle taking that same pride in a job well done as my dad had all those years.

That night as I found myself full of basketball, food, and great memories of serving my dad that day, The Lord began to unfold and show me the reason my dad took pride in the lawn and didn't want to entrust someone else to do it. I came to realize that he took pride in it because of all the things he had to sacrifice for our family to buy that house in 1986. It was also pride in the character he had in that God trusted him to take care of the house and yard work because it was gift from the Lord.

What is the "lawn" God has put in front of you? Sometimes it's a major jungle to start, but the maintenance of it will be easier to up-keep if we work at it every day, every week, and not lose sight of the fact that it's a true gift from God. You have the talents and resources to make it look immaculate. Sometimes He gives you help, so don't rob others of the chance to serve God as they help you because that *is* their calling as well.

We have all made sacrifices in our lives, and we still have many more in front of us, but we can meet them with joy, and the peace of God's hand is all over our life. We can take pride in the Lord as we take care of the "lawns" he puts before us if we…

JUST CHILL!

Lennon and I

My family

Just Chill

"I'm older now, I'm seeking shelter Against the Wind"
Against The Wind - Bob Seger

Chapter 13

Why's & What If's

When you have been through dark times like cancer, divorce, the loss of a loved one or a job, there's always those moments when you ask, "Why did that happen?" and "What If I had done this instead of that?" Those doubts and regrets can be detrimental in your faith. Faith in God's plan-A is believing that what He's promised us will happen even when we can't see anything moving.

So many of us have those stories when just one morning things all fall apart or come together. God is constantly at work in our lives, even if we don't see it. I don't believe in luck or coincidence. In my understanding of God's word, everything belongs to God, and everything comes from God. We don't have to recognize that for it to be true.

– – – –

Looking back on the "I wish I knew then what I know now" moments will drive us crazy. It will hold you in that place where you can't see any growth, and you can't grow more by allowing the shackles of guilt, sin and regret to hold you back.

The truth is that if we didn't go through those things, we wouldn't have learned what we know now. So the "why's" and "what if's" should be more about, *Why aren't you letting it go? What if you did move on and let God shape your character into who He meant for you to be?*

If we learn the lessons in the valleys of our past, then it wasn't in vein. The Bible tells us in Mark 9:9 that God doesn't reveal things at times we think we should be receiving them because we aren't spiritually ready to handle it. He puts us back in the incubator so that we can learn the lessons and catch our breath, so when the veil is lifted it will be an "Ah Ha" moment that sticks, and the only question then is "Why didn't I see it that way before?" Let me answer that for you now: YOU WEREN'T READY!

There are still things we will always be waiting for, but the momentum of what God helps us build comes from just trusting Him in every step. Instead of praying, "God change me," or "Lord, if it's your will," it should be, "God thank you for what you are doing to transform me now for what is to come," or "Lord pour into me what I need for where you are taking me and make those people and situations ready to receive it."

I know it's hard to let go of the pain and the wrong actions in our lives, and I'm not here to tell you how to pray, but I know I've seen in my own life that by speaking in faith God shows Himself to me and things turn out better than I could have ever imagined. The phrase, "God will change the situation or change you," is very spot one. He's changing you right now. His plan will blow you away because we can't out-dream God.

Finally, as you begin to let go of the past—it's good to point out that for many, myself included—we believe it's our lot in life to suffer for Jesus, but that is the opposite of what He promises. He wants us to completely surrender, and while we may have ramifications for what's happened, you don't have to carry that weight and guilt. If God has forgiven and forgotten, then we have to let it go so that we prosper in our hearts and soul. He is preparing something for you, and you can't hold onto what's coming if you are still holding on to what's dead and done.

Plus, the key all along to what's holding you back is to let go so that you can prove to God and others you have learned to JUST CHILL.

McCartney and I

Quotes of Endorsement

"Ace is one of the great radio guys I've had the honor to know in my career. No Matter what station I've seen him at God has used Him in major ways and I love seeing a fellow Bama boy serving the Lord in this way."

Mac Powell from Third Day

"Ace is transparent and authentic and understands the power of story and the hunger for human connection through our words, music and the medium of radio. I'm thankful to call him a friend and excited for this next chapter to unfold."

Darren Mulligan from We Are Messengers

I remember being a young, scared kid making the rounds around the country to introduce myself and my music to radio stations. It's what you do when you're a new artist. Talk about intimidating! Well, some of those first radio people I met in the beginning are still friends to this day. Ace is one of those guys. We've shared meals and stories as both of our careers have progressed. We've shared a common love for music and faith. I don't doubt that "Just Chill" will be filled with his unique perspective, life stories, and lessons learned along the way.

~Matthew West/Christian Aritst

CPSIA information can be obtained
at www.ICGtesting.com
Printed in the USA
LVHW020036130819
627343LV00011B/678/P

9 781644 265727